ALSO BY SAMUEL RAHBERG

Ice Break: Poems about Change
Enduring Ministry: Toward a Lifetime of Christian Leadership
The Gospels in Poem and Image (with artist Natalie Adebiyi)
The Way Forward: A Collection of Benedictine Inspirations (editor)

SHADOEMS

SHADOW WORK THROUGH POEMS

Samuel Rahberg

Natalie Adebiyi

AETOS PUBLICATIONS
SAINT PAUL, MINNESOTA

For those we love,
beyond all names and pronouns.

CONTENTS

ACKNOWLEDGEMENTS

With thanks to the family and friends who accept the whole of me,
sometimes before I find the courage to do so myself. Especially Natalie,
who wraps her artistic talent around my questions, and Michael Sirany
and Victor Klimoski, who help me find
language for such things.

INTRODUCTION

Poetry escorts us to thresholds between the familiar and the unknown within us, guiding us into liminal spaces where we encounter things previously avoided, unrecognized, or more complicated than we had imagined. These moments may feel like rare shimmers on a sea of humdrum attention and assumption, yet life is constantly offering invitations to something more.

A poem equips us to accept these invitations, urging us to pause and stretch the boundaries of our awareness. Through its lines, we discover beauty to savor, ambiguities to explore, and stirrings of new wisdom whispering in our ear.

Jungian analyst James Hollis helps illuminate the significance of such thresholds. "The human ego is not capable of full awareness . . . ," he writes, "It's not capable of healing itself. It has to come to terms with those parts of itself that are operating in forms that are contrary to its intentionality."

Hollis is referring to what Jung called the "Shadow," those aspects of ourselves we might prefer to deny or that exist outside our current perspective. Shadow work is a moral task, calling us to bring into consciousness the truths we might resist. Sometimes, this is a disruptive summons to greatness; other times, it reveals parts of us that seem at odds with our values. In the context of Shadow work, healing is about learning to befriend these tensions, embracing a self that is larger than our present ability to fully comprehend.

For me, the most constructive understanding of Shadow does not frame it primarily as a source of evil or an untouchable dimension of human nature. Instead, I appreciate a view of Shadow as a realm of what lies beyond our current capacity to see—the hidden aspects of who we are and how we relate to the world, operating at a subconscious level but shaping our lives in profound ways. As I read Hollis, I hear an invitation to healing through the ongoing practice of becoming more conscious about these unseen parts and their effects.

This practice is not about judgment or self-condemnation. It is about integration through acknowledging the parts of ourselves we are inclined to ignore: our fears, biases, hidden motives, or unfulfilled longings. But also facing those interior impulses toward compassion or courage so intense they intimidate us. We do not name them to banish them, but to learn from them and to grow in freedom.

Shadow Work

Daily life is full of threshold experiences that bring the Shadow into view. Every poem in this collection is written in the hope that it can become both an affirmation of and active inquiry into this possibility. These poems reflect moments of turning toward reality, seeing more clearly, shedding unworkable presumptions, and recalibrating to integrate what once was hidden.

Because shadow work calls us home to the parts of ourselves we tend to overlook, ignore, or repress, we need tools to navigate this terrain. For me, writing has proven the most reliable form. Poetry's creative process insists that I re-examine and reframe my relationship to experiences that might otherwise remain unnoticed or underappreciated.

Shadow work, for me, has meant befriending difficult realities like chronic pain, melancholy, loss, and transitions such as empty nesting and vocational shifts. But it has also been about befriending emergence— moments of unexpected contentment, inspiration, and the unraveling of self-limiting narratives. These poems testify to the healing dignity of struggle and discovery, echoing the Scripture, "The truth shall set you free." More truth, more freedom.

Writing Toward Emergence

Writing these poems often felt like fumbling in the dark, each one a touchstone on the way toward expanded perspective. Writing and revising allowed me to practice bringing the unknown and unwelcomed into view. Old patterns of avoidance had become habitual, and poetry offered a way to tease these truths into the light. Each stanza became a small chance to refocus and reframe things in ways that might translate some bit of wisdom into daily life.

Poems are uniquely suited for this work because they exist at the threshold of clarity and mystery. Not every facet of unknowing or unwelcoming can be fully articulated, for the Shadow dwells beyond our current awareness. Yet, in their attempt to name an experience authentically, poems become natural companions for exploring the Shadow.

The Invitation

This collection is for those walking along the edge of their own Shadow and wanting to nourish their sense of curiosity and solidarity. These poems are companions for times when the world's ambiguity feels overwhelming, when the inner life stirs with uncertainty and contradiction. I hope they offer you invitations to pause at your own thresholds and linger long enough for something new to emerge.

The readers most likely to find this collection meaningful are living into questions like mine:

- How do I engage this season of life more fully, being increasingly honest about the limitations within and around me?
- How do I wrestle more creatively with the rumblings and contradictions of my interior life?
- What grace do I need to accept discomfort and struggle not as interruptions or anomalies, but as dignified aspects of the human journey—just as valuable as moments of ease and contentment?

Shadoems in Eight Parts

The collection is organized into eight sections, each exploring a facet of shadow work:

On Shadow
Befriending the tensions between the seen and unseen,
the known and unknown.

Shimmers
Fleeting glimpses of beauty and insight as constant
invitations to something more.

Fumblings
Reflections on the clumsy, vulnerable, imperfect process of facing the
Shadow.

Meditations
Quiet ways to linger in ambiguity, savoring questions without rushing
toward answers.

Contradictions
Explorations of the wholistic interplay between opposites—
joy and sorrow, clarity and confusion.

Labors
Reminders of the dignity of human work and the formation
that accompanies it.

Longings
Stirring desires for purpose, connection, and mutual understanding
all too often unspoken.

Wonders
Encounters with awe and reverence that leave us humbled
and free.

The Nature of Creativity and Freedom

There's a risk in over-psychologizing Shadow work, so let me offer a metaphor from one poem in the section *On Shadow*. "Averted Gaze" studies one of nature's great mysteries—that the human eye is hardwired to perceive celestial wonders best when looking slightly away. Some stars seem dim, even imperceivable, when viewed directly. This is because our eyes rely on distinct photoreceptor cells in the retina. Cones detect color in bright light and are in the center of the retina. Rods, on the other hand, are sensitive to dim light and are concentrated in our peripheral vision.

Harnessing this peripheral vision, ancient astronomers taught stargazers to look just to the side of a dim object in the heavens in order to see it more clearly. Something similar is true in shadow work:

"See with eye's edge
when things lack brightness."

We were made for this. To realize freedom, however, we must employ a bit of creativity in how we choose to see. The artwork in this collection, by the talented Natalie Adebiyi, can help us—her charcoal interpretations serve as visual invitations to further reflection, evoking our capacity to perceive things at the edges.

Closing Encouragement

If, at any point while reading, you find yourself encountering something that feels like too much or too soon, go gently with yourself. Shadow work unfolds best with patience and compassionate attention.

May these poems serve as companions for you as you navigate your own thresholds. Whether you are facing loss, transition, or simply the quiet unease of uncertainty, may you discover dignity in struggle, beauty in ambiguity, and wisdom waiting to emerge from the shadows.

First Sunday in Lent

I
ON SHADOW

befriending the tensions between
the seen and unseen, the known and unknown

Shadoems

Some poems stand
at Shadow's edge,
eyes squinting
over a candle's flicker.
If Shadow holds
all that is still unseen,
uncensored, or unwelcomed,
and if we long to see real
wholeness and homecoming,
what, then, is a brave poem
called to do?

To reach for words
To provide margin for doubt
    and disorientation
To exercise longing
To venerate connectedness
To re-examine things that always were
    and now no longer work
To communicate the
    otherwise unspoken
To stand in the public eye
To test perspectives
To be let go
To keep planting seeds
To shape memories
To suffer translation
To cross generations
To say again and again,
    We are alive.

Averted Gaze

Even with the urban glow
two hours at your back
and the cosmos,
deep and black,
enveloping
Earth as a pebble,
there are stars we cannot see
by looking directly.
Venus and Orion's Belt
are obvious enough
at this end of light years,
but dimmer wonders
celestial
come into view only
when you look
just beside them.
Ancients and astronomers
pass on this wisdom,
for stargazing and for life—
See with eye's edge
when things lack brightness.
We were made
for such beholding,
our seeing sharpened
as we ease
into awareness.

Pushing Clouds

Loss rolls in
and lingers

Like a sheet drawn
across the sun

Changing
to dusk

An otherwise
bright enough day.

There is no
fighting, willing

Or pretending
the shadows away.

Trust the light
for now unseen.

The rest is
pushing clouds.

Peripheral Vision

A frosted window
remains a still frame
of skeletal limbs
only as long as our focus
is too little or too much.
We can presume
we've seen these woods before.
Or miss the panorama
when we've dialed in
on a single open knot
in a high-broken branch.
Relax your seeing,
let it widen, trust
peripheral vision.
There are scurries, flutters,
and more signs of sentinels
that have been there all along.

Shadow Work Entries — The First
on the assumption that life's inexplicabilities might,
in effect, become a constellation of invitations

I.   Ear Tired
One spiritual companion tells me he doesn't like talking about
himself. Some days, weary of the stories I hear myself telling, I
think he may be more wise than not. But people ask and I say
too much because I'm tired of pretending.

II.   Qigong
"Smile!" says the kind old master. "Take in happiness, joy, and
peace from the Universe!" "Effin' hell," says I, the overweight
and tensed-up student. "You've just précised the blockages
that made me desperate enough to be here."

III.   Black Dog
A snarling black dog, wearing a deceptively friendly blue
bandana, charged me on my morning walk. His fierce brother
and shouting owner chased close behind. Do I run? Do I lunge
barking back at him, like the equanimous monk I once heard
about? This day, I wait, look at him gently, and wish the owner
good morning. That seems as much energy as I can muster.

IV.   Sensory Night
I haven't figured out what comes after the fighting
dissatisfaction phase. Clearly, there's some need to clarify my
"why" and re-engage the world, but I lack sufficient
wherewithal. If commentators are right that the Dark Night of
the Senses purges one's dependence upon consoling feelings
and experiences, perhaps I could take this numbness to mean
that I have attained something.

V.   Side Owl
Huge and silent she crosses way up in the rafters of the maple
trees on a wet, cool, Wales-like morning. I'd have never sensed
her on purpose. I just happened to be watching when she
swooped into peripheral vision, like wisdom dropping in near
a whiff of paying attention.

VI. Projecting Shadow

Someone on the internet said we project our Shadow onto people and situations so we can better fight what we refuse to accept in ourselves. They probably said other things, but I was too consumed by my mind's deluge of personal examples to notice.

VII. Resisting What?

What am I so afraid of befriending in myself that I would rather live out lopsided swings from over-engaged against-energy, to complete disengagement, then thrashing back?

For starters . . .

1. That I am intimidated by the way my "no" unlocks people's disappointment;
2. That I don't want to believe failure is so integral to life's program;
3. That the intensity of anger seems more palatable than the sadness it tends to hide;
4. That, in the struggle to prove my own worth, I tend to squeeze out inefficient and disruptive moments of contentment;
5. That I will never catch up to my own dreaming;
6. Etc., etc.

Shadow Work Entries — The Second

VII.   SAN IVAN DE LA CRUZ
I swear the icon said IVAN in capital Latin letters before I started sleeping under his watch. I presumed Ivan was some Russian staretz and continued an entirely separate quest to find words for my Dark Night of the Soul. I kept wandering off to other places as if the next library or hyperlink could help me make sense of my experience. But by day three, I realized the letters in my own room read Juan, as in St. John of the Cross.

IX.   Fear Filing
When someone asked me to explain my 30-year-old filing system, even I gasped at how many clicks and terabytes I invest in my defense against being caught flat-footed.

X.   Crime and Punishment
Raskolnikov nearly broke under his evolution of morality. Over 492 pages, it was love in the end—not power—that began to redeem him. As I try to claim a center of authority less defined by others' whims and conventions, what makes me think I would require any less?

XI.   Incrementally Conscious
Shadow work will not be harnessed, driven, or controlled. Wait. Lean into resistance. Accept indirect truth as it bends, often disruptively, toward freedom.

XII.   New Playlist
Within the first three notes of enrapturing guitar and sultry piano, I woke from my task and came home to my soul. Dirty Blues.

XIII. Choosing

Every retreat, whether moments or days, means missing out on worthy somethings and saying no to significant someones. But it's precisely this terrible risk in choosing that reminds us we're alive.

XIV. Odie

Two months ago, Odie the blonde, neutered barn cat disappeared. That hurt like other instant absences—his brother Garfield, Mozzy the tuxedoed mouser, three chickens plucked off one at a time, and then an entire flock lost to a single weasel. Whether Odie finally outran the eagle, owl, coyote, or giant Tom, he returned today scratched deep and hungry for three bowls of food.

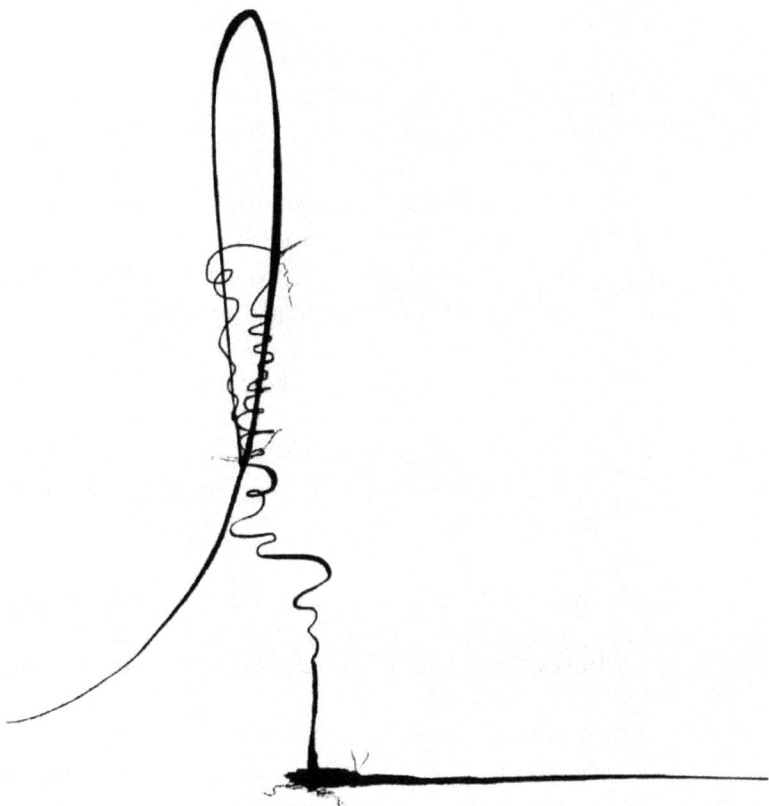

Shadow Work Entries — The Third

XVI. Kwik Trip

Apparently, HR at Kwik Trip wasn't impressed that I safely towed a trailer through 42 states and eight provinces, because I didn't get the job trucking groceries to convenience stores at night. Nor did my 25 years of experience help me make it past the second interview for assisting manager positions in either of two towns. When I checked in to my motel the night I got that news, I waited behind a troupe of wrestling dwarves. (The manager was trying to activate a new American Express card while the assistant renegotiated a room on first floor, since Manuel could not do stairs, but Rickie could shoulder a mammoth suitcase and scurry right on up with the others). Eventually, I got my key, checked twice for bedbugs, and opened the shades. In keeping with the day's absurdity, I found myself squinting beneath the bright lights of a Kwik Trip station immediately next door.

XVII. Reconciling to What Is

"To live wakefully is to live in full awareness of this, our human situation." Check (painfully so).

"To live well is to reconcile ourselves to it, and try to realize whatever excellence we can." Growth mindset?

   (Matthew Crawford in *Shop Class as Soulcraft: An Inquiry into the Value of Work*)

XVIII. Contours of Exhaustion

If exhaustion is the new normal, I challenge us to become more articulate about its contours. Bone weary or bored? Futiled or dissatisfied? Hard worked or disappointed? Conditions of your own making or your inheritance? Overwhelm at suffering—yours or the world's? Claiming nuance brings us one step closer to imagining remedy.

XIX. Passive Tension

Lucas taught a yoga principle I want to live—time under passive tension. Real, lasting change means learning to breathe . . . ease into the right intensity . . . and stay with it.

XX.   Power

Memes would have us believe that Einstein called compound interest the most powerful force in the Universe. And that Gandhi preferred unconditional love. Perhaps real life suffers their interplay.

XXI.   Universe

When the spring sun makes you tip your head up and close your eyes, or the sun sets over the fields in a way that makes you breathe deep the holy of autumn, then, then . . . you belong to the cosmos.

Here Be Dragons

When I was 13, I sat down in the TV room with my grandfather as he was watching *Die Hard*. He didn't say no, so I stayed and took in my first R-rated film after years of John Wayne and *Star Trek* (the original). These were the years my folks drove a station wagon to a box store and rented a VHS machine with two tapes—one PG for the four kids and one R for them. I noticed that *Die Hard* (and probably my folk's movies) built on similar building blocks to all the PG stories: epic journeys, good vs. evil, and constant moral reconsideration.

Nearly 40 years later, something in the market and our culture seems to drift toward more shadowed explorations of these elements. As I catch myself binging an MA-rated series about pirates (streamed entirely without the need for a station wagon or rewind machine), I wonder what that's about. What's pulling me in? Why *this* story? How is it enticing my lesser-known parts of myself into view?

The first hook is as obvious as it is profitable. The media industry has mastered ways to grab our primal attractions to enviable freedom of personal and sexual expression, adrenaline pumping adventure, struggle between right and wrong (at least what seems so at first), and some promise of meaning and significance that comes with a character summoned to a quest. We buy all that for the initial rush.

We *keep* buying, however, for the slow burn. The media industry knows they must burrow in and sustain a more complex grip on our inner worlds. They have learned that we keep clicking "Next episode" only when they successfully craft storylines that begin to read *us* and refuse to let us go, ones that dwell in the constant clash of expectations and character development well beneath the plot line. It's these inner churnings underneath the mythic purpose that keeps us latched on—perhaps because they bring our own becoming into view.

Pirates, apparently, can show us the way. Acknowledging the weight of responsibility for doing what others cannot accomplish, alongside the weariness from constant compromise. A villain expanding our understanding of integrity. Stings of betrayal revealing commitment to deeper loyalty. Setting down fears of being measured by others to begin defining one's own legitimacy—even when the world fights back. A self-actualized Anima saying, "I find there is an inverse relationship between one's happiness and one's concern for appearance." Then bearing healing as mother, wife, and mistress. The emotional catharsis of yielding to and consummating love. Casting aside shame. Learning to let go of what was created in response to loss.

I am not advocating that we consume any dark story that comes along. Instead, I mean to encourage us to notice when a narrative is moving us and then welcome whatever is helping us integrate parts of ourselves that have been living in exile.

If we find artful complexity that causes us to expand our self-awareness and re-examine our orientation for this difficult age, and if that story intends to form us through the ancient tradition of tragic tales, then let us follow those storytellers and set sail for the dragons.

Soul Collage – The First

Drummer

I am the one who removes masks and sets energy free.
I give you a drum beat steady as the sun and river flow.
I want harmony in and beyond life. Practice here and now.

Well-Aged Joy

I am the one whose eyes glimmer today.
I give you freedom to savor memories that fade,
    grateful and more whole because of them.
The trees have seen it all—at least two generation's worth.

Beleaguered

I am the one who is weary.
I give you permission to taste the water before you feel
    refreshed.
I want to sit still in the morning light.

Soul Collage – The Second

Brotherhood

I am the one who gazes into this world,
    connected to another time.
I bring you a brotherhood of honorable souls.
I want you to remember your courage,
    to stand in the sun and be seen.

Loyal Burro

I am the one who childishly labels someone an ass.
I want you to remember she is wholly her own.
Trust the kindness of a useful and loyal burro.

Light Water

I am the one who stands unseen until needed.
I see you from above and below the waterline.
I give you the stamina forged by fierce landscapes.

Bonsai Life

I am the one who is patient enough to welcome life from death.
I graft bouquets onto old limbs.
I want you to appreciate arts that are not yours to do.

II
SHIMMERS
fleeting glimpses of beauty and insight
that remind us of constant invitations
to something more

Beach Problem
for Peter

When dawn rises blood-orange
over an island ridge,
the coffee is finished,
and the deep blue Jeep
winds up the trailhead

When your hike eases
downhill 1,200 feet
past bright spiders,
towering rum trees,
and hidden falls with petroglyphs

When you step through
the nearshore door
of flora and fauna
into a vista wide enough
to hold the sun's rise and set

When a canvas of colors
breaks upon white sand,
only a sailboat to see you
sharing tuna sandwiches
and beer still cold

Then do you know
what the problem
with the beach is?
In this other worldly moment,
I should hope not.

For Love of Morning

Maybe it's bird song
before the traffic drum,
sensing the ease
of a home still asleep,
or memories of that first step
into crisp mountain air
beside the ancient trout stream.
There's also something about
prelude to expectations,
before punching in to sort things
and keep pressing forward.
I smell the first hints of French roast
and they help me wonder
about such things in the wee hour
sanctuary of a day.
All this summons me
to set the pot and turn in
early the night before,
to wake gladly before my alarm,
and to wander between words
and silence and movement
in wholly essential moments
ante meridiem,
beginning to metabolize life
before and after.

Taste of Morning

While a person might
lurch out of bed,
hit the lights
and tear open the day,
morning is far better spent
building flavor.

Heat the skillet,
slowly warming the oil
– but not to smoke.
Sauté onions to clear and crisp,
stirring single next ingredients
only when a coalesced aroma
has released from the last.
Wait, wait . . .

Better in dark hours
we warm stiff limbs,
layer in a prayer,
a reading. Steady now,
while this profile
begs for a simmer.
Stay still . . .

Let subtle notes
and complex ones
settle out and blend,
reducing toward
this day's nourishing,
delicious
beginning.

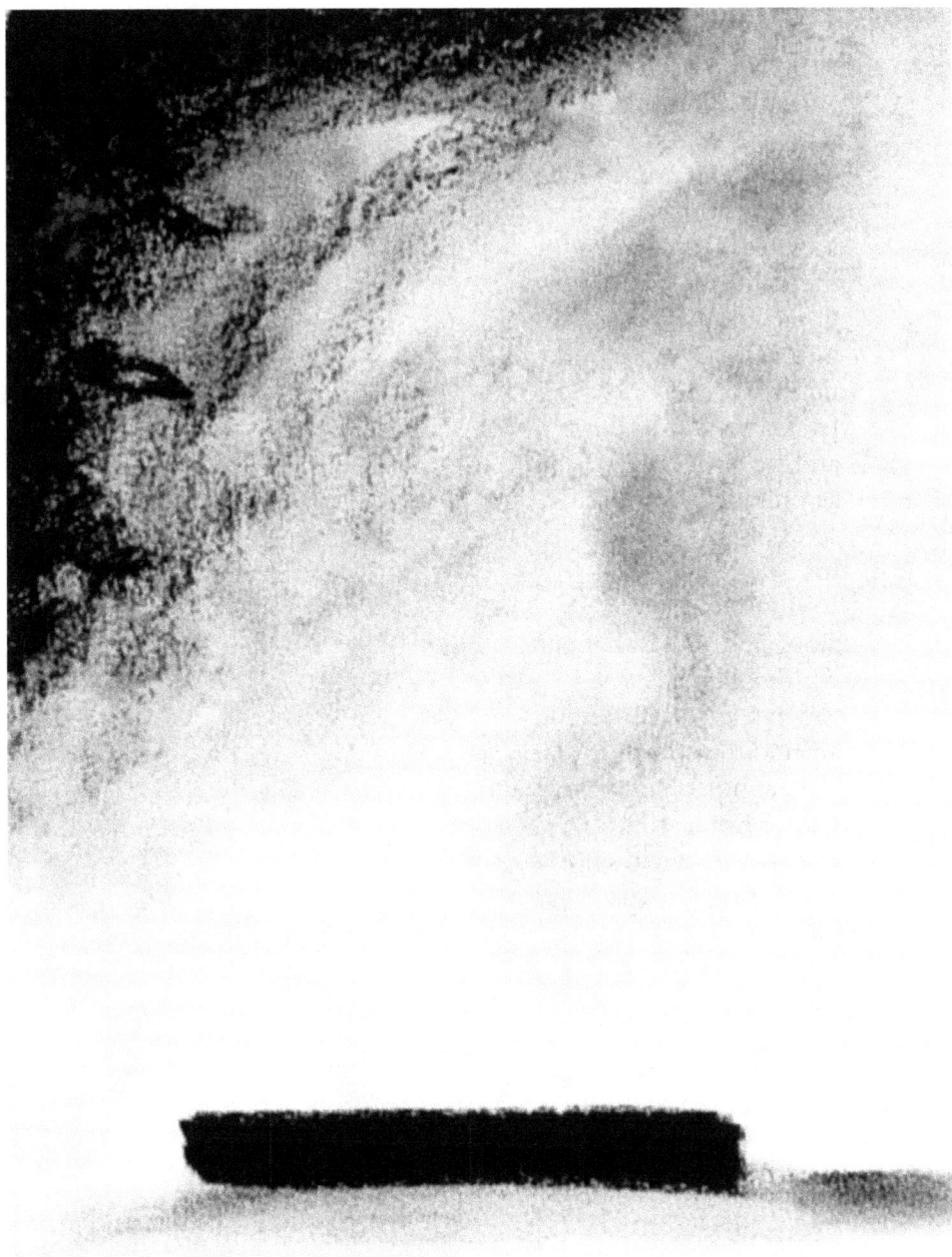

Loon Song

A single, haunting tremelo
rides the cool breeze
of an overcast morning,
announcing presence.
Next comes silence,
then a gentle gust
tipping night-wet leaves
into a patter of second
rains onto the brick walk.
Last, a refrain of hoots
and wavering calls
as prelude to sunrise,
set the mood
for awakening soul.
In this place,
alongside all that happens
within old walls
to wrap words and minds
around the search for God,
loon song comes as invitation,
Lake Sagatagan's
not-so-whispered chorus,
wondering when
—if—
you'll pause to listen,
listen.

Dawn Chorus — Jazz Edition

Sax and chimes shimmer awake
stiff limbs noticing edges,
playing with flow and response.
What language do they speak
and from where?
Light, flexible touch . . .
study the gift of supporting voices.
Ever just play the tightest or
fastest notes you can hit?
What of the music is predictable?
What must be new every time?
Make way for the mellow of Santana,
sipping turmeric tea.
What is it like to misplace notes
so infrequently?
To take the lead in conversation
or welcome a flute's interlude?
What makes the trumpet commanding
and who dares
while trombones hold up the floor?
At what mystical point
do musicians play subconsciously,
the clean, tight sound of the single note,
rising with others into
brightness of day?

Geese on the Morning Sky

A lone honk sounds off
from the lake's eastern rim,
ripples into a handful of calls closer,
then swells into thousands
directly overhead.
So loud is the crescendo
that even those who slept
through the peel of abbey bells
leap to their windows
and duck under the thunder
of Canada Geese so low.
They crowd the sky unstoppably,
single voices fused into
one trembling roar until,
just as suddenly,
a diminuendo of stragglers
gives way to one last honk
dotting an edge of their wake.

With You
for Daisy
"Be strong and courageous . . . "
(Joshua 1:9)

What is it
that makes you
hesitate,
the unlit corner
at the bottom of the stairs
that compels you
to give up,
to go around,
or to pat down the wall
for a light switch?
When you find yourself
at that edge,
giggling nervously
and heart pounding,
remember
this is only one
of many dark places
you will need to go.
Slow down.
Listen for the whisper,
the one that always
accompanies you,
Be strong.
Be courageous.
Your God is with you
wherever you will go.

Living Waters

We are pails of many colors
shapes and marvelous designs,
searching for somethings—anythings
that will fill us to the brim.
But we share one unfortunate flaw:
we are pails of many holes.
The leaks of imperfection
worsen by hurts and fears
until more is lost than
gained by our fetching.
"Pour life into me," we cry,
and when all passes through
we lament, "If only this or that,
a bit more and faster, then
I would have life to give."
All the while something
quietly wells up,
a flood rising all around
seeps into every pail,
entering first low openings.
Now within and around
still rising,
a tide consumes the world.
Higher it flows, fills pails
outside in,
up to the brim, then beyond.
Feigning emptiness we miss this—
We are holy pails submerged
in living waters.

III
FUMBLINGS

reflections on the clumsy, vulnerable,
imperfect process of facing the Shadow

Happy Birthday Dear [. . .]

for Ezra

The fault line of pronouns and naming conventions,
at least for this dad, does not cross ideologies and debate.
It is technical difficulty. Mechanical impasse.
Twenty years of hardwiring.

Today, on my own child's birthday, I don't quite know
how to sing. Or at least I do not know
whether I dare try for fear of crying. I am choked back
by the physical inability to address him/them.

He has claimed a new gender and name
that does not yet register with their lifetime
of my fierce affection, loyalty,
and abiding.

Old handles still saturate every memory
with shorthand for who they are (were),
something I called out loud that made him turn
at home, in a crowd, wherever I reached for his uniqueness.

I chose that first name,
imbued it with sincere hopes
and the deepest meaning I knew at the time.
He seeks an identity beyond those bounds.

Today, a photo of tiny shoes appeared on my feed
—red, blue, and green with white laces—
insensitive to the fact that I was driving this child home,
freshly mind-bended and stuttering a new name.

I haven't learned to do this yet,
so I'm starting by mouthing the words.
Like changing the nickname on accounts.
The speed dial label. Email contact lists.

How I introduce myself as a father of [. . .]
How his mother and I practice in private.
I imagine this will be a deliberate,
"Good night [. . .]," and "I love you [. . .],"

Over and over until years give way
and "Hey [. . .]!" comes as instinctually
as my unequivocal yes to this person
—the same yes that remains beyond words anyway.

Lost Wallet

That stripped down feeling.
Beyond embarrassment
    with the cashier.
The pat down,
The pocket plunge,
The rifling,
The exploding unpack
    of everything.
Car seats and consoles.
The maybe-I-missed-it (agains).
The call for help
    from a wayside rest.
Kind, but nothing turned up
    and call back tomorrow.
The space between.
Undocumented.
Afraid of being caught
    or robbed of myself.
The distraction
    and waiting.
Retracing steps
    and waiting.
The no-help like,
    "Where did you have it last?"
The bubbly Gen-Z-er
    who assures me she'll look,
    but didn't ask for my phone number.
More waiting at the mercy
    of strangers.
Like the maintenance guy
    who noticed it unprompted and
    chose to return it.
All this is encounter
    with what is really lost,
a disruption to privilege,
    security, identity.

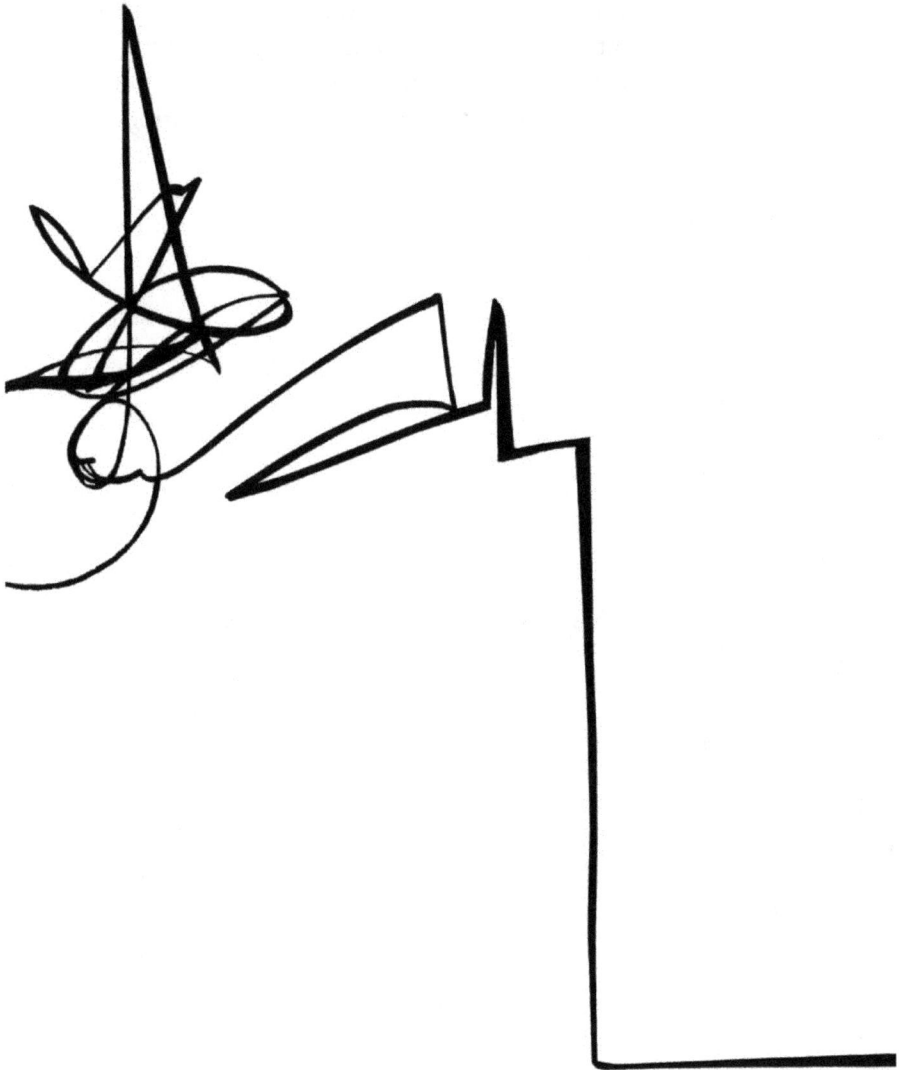

My Nature

What in me finds human voices an interruption to my experiences of nature? Like tourists at my cathedrals, planes over my national parks, roars of traffic next to my lake, too much family at my reunions, too many patrons at my libraries. There may be times and settings for real solitude, but rare are the occasions I actually have a right to my indignation. Because I am just as much the one on the plane, in the car, speaking too loudly, or running a chainsaw near someone else's trail. The art of awakening is coming home to what is *also* true, being present, present without judgment.

Aw, Shit

The moment we own
the familiar stench
of wet organic waste
is when we stop
to lift our shoe,
to look at the sole
in a way we never do.
There it all is,
smeared into our tread
except for the stains
we've probably tracked
as far as we have come.
Better had we left
footsteps along some
concrete sidewalk
or hidden in the grass.
But no, this trail
is long and cruel—
the threshold, the carpet,
the tile, the stairs, and even
the place for prayer.
So we blurt out
exactly what we find,
compelled to scrub and study
on hands and knees
the cost of a single
mindless step.

Tinnitus

Coffee buzz
third cup
eyes screen dulled.
Chronic kinks
clenched jaw
both wrists stiff.
Hemorrhoids
—the bad kind—
Restless legs
back sore
long broken sleep.
Body rings
tinnitusly.
May be time
to listen.

Do Light

The Fraggle Rock puppet show
featured Doozers,
folks like me who
just kept working.
To pause was to hesitate
on life's one purpose.

By what measure
might today's Doozer
be convinced
that stillness, breathing,
spaciousness
are key to worthy work?

When I can slow
down enough
to wonder,
the closest I get is
"Be light."
"Do light."

For light moves so fast
it seems steady,
rests through night
to return anew,
illuminates all things
that make work possible.

Until motion and stillness
share a rhythm,
any work will fade.
Be light, then,
with the same fullness
you Doozer.

My Neighbor's Good

The grievance that fuels
this age of media profits
is not likely to fade
as long as it drives
people to the polls.
This tragedy extends beyond
toxic public discourse.
Our shared failings
compromise real lives
when convictions
about truth and freedom
were forged in resentment
—not dignity.
Untruth drives us away from
wholehearted love of God
through one another.
Maybe the way forward
begins by taking up
the old fumbled question,
"Yeah, but who is my neighbor?"
For as long as the answer remains,
"None. Mine. These."
we cannot afford to yield
anything to "Them."
God of Abundance,
reorient us all
with the clarity of practical love,
a kinship inextricably bound
by our common good.

Counting Pronouns
for Dei

Easy, please, with the
condescension,
having told me
to use new pronouns
for my child of eighteen years.
You might as well have said:

"Count to 10 as fast as you can,
swap * for 2 and @ for 8,
reverse 5 and 6—
no redoes, no repeats.
If you love me,
just get it right."

I hold a fear that when I slip,
you might push away.
Your name, your nouns
pass unthinkingly over my lips
as echoes and signs of long-practiced
heart connection.

Those sounds live in muscle memory,
exposing the hardwiring
fused around your first coos,
shouted over fields and crowds,
impulses that reached out to you,
as surely as they used to turn your head.

Even then, know that my deep care
penetrates your gender expression
and any words you choose.
What I want most for you
is to come home to your truest self
wholly, unconditionally loved.

Remember all this, dear one,
when my words appear clumsy—
I am still practicing
1*34657@910 . . .
and I'll keep counting
until you hear you belong.

IV
MEDITATIONS
quiet invitations to linger in ambiguity,
savoring questions without
rushing toward answers

Sitting Meditation

Notice the breath move in
and feel that breath
as it passes cooly down,
enters lungs,
fills chest and stomach.

Watch the breath released,
now warmed by its passage,
rising up and out,
somewhat faster than before.

Rest with the breath
for its moment between
and begin again.

The ear may notice sound,
and the mind may search it out,
wondering, explaining.
Without judgment,
without upset,
come back to the sensation
of each breath.
There is no need to push or control.
Simply let breath
anchor your awareness.

The mind may drift to fantasy,
memory, thoughts of the day,
to worry, lists of things to do.
Gently, firmly come back.
Follow the coolness
toward the rhythm of breath.
Let your attention
be light and easy.

Opinions may swell,
preferences and judgments
may come and go.
Just notice,
bring awareness back
to what is most vivid in breath.
How freeing to do only this.

The body may ache
or express tension, discomfort.
Notice in a friendly way,
then ride waves of breath
in and down,
up and out.
Rest in the between space.

Stay with pure sensation,
home in this body,
this moment.

When attention still wanders,
can you celebrate
the noticing, the returning?

This, this is making ready
to receive whatever comes,
to hold feelings of peace
or sadness
without judgment,
breathing into all things,
breathing through all things.

This ends the Sitting Meditation.

Rules for Stretching
with thanks to Lucas

During a 5-minute hold
of "Thread the Needle,"
What?
(Seated with back to the wall
left ankle crossed over bent right knee)
You've got to be kidding me.
(Hands reaching around right shin
interlacing fingers and
pulling the knee)
Wait, this works.
The teacher reassures us—
as much for life as stretching.

Breathe in through your nose
to the count of four . . .
Easy enough.
breathe out through your mouth
making a "Haaah" sound
to the count of eight . . .
I'll try to trust the process.
This practice disarms
the greatest barrier
to a good stretch—
your own nervous system.
Yes, yes I do have a system of nervousness.
Breathing relaxes the body's instinct
to use tension to protect itself.

Remain in this pose
and keep breathing . . .
giving yourself time enough
to ease defenses and find
your stretch beneath the tension.
My God. That sounds like Cliffs Notes
for my 30 years of therapy. How?
How do I live like this?

Rule #1?
Wet Noodle
Muscles stretch better when relaxed.
Breathe . . . breathe . . .
I want to believe there is something deeper than
constant grasping for security.

Rule #2?
Seven Out of Ten Intensity
Too much, you risk injury.
Too little, you lack healthy challenge.
I wonder what might blossom
if my all-or-nothing were re-calibrated.

Rule #3?
Time Under Passive Tension
To grow daily, meet or beat the hold time.
Refer to rule #1 and #2.
I'm holding, I'm holding
and hoping you're about to say,
"Switch sides."

This ends the Stretching Meditation.

Prayer in Motion

Hands Push the Sky
With heart, soul, and mind,
I honor the Holy Trinity.
In truth and freedom,
I encourage those in need.
Watching my thinking, feeling, and body,
I let go of whatever is illusion.
At ease in the Spirit,
I entrust myself to Divine Wisdom.

Following the Palm
Following the path of Christ's love,
I journey toward union with God.

Scissor the Fists
Embracing genuine humility,
I contemplate Christ's teachings.

Clearing the Mind
Releasing burdens past and future,
I am open to the Eternal in this moment.

Bow and Arrow
Surrendering to what is Good and Beautiful,
I am wholly enough.

Turning Rivers and Sea & Heaven and Earth
With groundedness of forest
and fluidity of stream,
I trust God's lovingkindness.
I set intentions wholeheartedly
and respond gracefully
to changing circumstance.

Omniscient Mind
In God's time,
all is revealed.

The Dharma Wheel
Continuously sharing the learning I have been given,
God's wisdom flows to others.

Emptying the Mind
Empty of shame and judgment,
I am full of wonder. Guided by the Gospel,
I work with joy.
Enlivened by the Spirit,
I become more and more like Christ.

Buddha's Bow & The Offering
Infused with the compassion of Christ,
I embrace all of Creation.
I accompany those in my path
toward deepening relationship with God.
Embodying the fruit of the Spirit,
I am without self-criticism,
without fear of others' opinions.
I am by nature child of God,
Beloved.
I am rooted in grace and brother to the Universe.
I abide in the Divine Presence.

This ends the Motion Meditation.

Bluff Meditation

This bluff is massive and beautiful
afar or nearby.
When the earth beneath you
reminds you to feel your body
or when the valley view
invites you to notice your breath,
kneel down upon the bluff's crown.
Press into its dignity, wholeness.
Let hidden layers of limestone,
compressing eons of leaves and earth,
uplift you with their majesty.
Bring them into yourself,
alive and unwavering.
Though light and seasons change
the bluff's appearance,
below its surface
calmness abides.
Stretch down your hands,
far enough to touch the river's song.
Listen to silence
reaching deeper
toward stillness, wisdom, resolve.
Whatever comes,
carry this bluff within.

This ends the Bluff Meditation.

Lovingkindness Meditation

White haired, wrinkled scalp,
gnarled fingers,
brown calloused feet,
a Cambodian elder glows
with lovingkindness.

She needs no words
for prayers embodied—
missing teeth, smiling joy,
bright-eyed gentleness,
blessings softly reaching.

She presses her hands together
and bows slowly to each one.
Without a whisper she conveys
a lifetime's meditation,
shining toward all beings—

May you be happy, healthy, and whole.
May you be protected from harm and free from fear.
May you and I live as one with inner peace and ease.

This ends the Lovingkindness Meditation.

Difficulties Meditation

Ease into the place of your body,
noticing what supports you,
the points of contact.
Let tensions drain down,
down through those points,
letting go thoughts and feelings.
Let breath be breath,
coming in and going out
like waves touching the shore,
smoothing the sand as they withdraw,
reaching again toward shore.
We don't expect anything else from waves.
We don't demand they come in faster or slower.
Just watch waves be waves
and breath be breath.

Find today's difficulty in you,
some physical pain or discomfort,
some unsettling emotion or feeling.
Pay attention with the same care you would
for a loved one experiencing the same.
Try identifying the feeling, saying,
"I notice something in me that is heavy, sharp,
or something that seems angry, sad, afraid, confused."
Give the sensation room to move.
What are you feeling now?
Where is your body reacting?
Meet the experience with kindness.
See if you can soften those difficulties
with tender breathes and gentleness.

These difficulties
would be hard for anyone.
Hold them with compassion,
without rushing.
Allow the feelings to be,
acknowledge them with curiosity.

Make contact with those feelings,
but not to the point of being overwhelmed.

Without pushing the difficulties away,
find something for which you are grateful.
Let it flow into your awareness
with gratitude and warmth.
Notice where you feel this in your body.
Spend some time here,
reflecting on things, people,
qualities for which you are grateful.
Don't fight remembering the difficulties.
Instead, allow soft breaths
and gently return to the good things,
the good people in your life.
Trust feelings to be fluid and dynamic,
breathing between the pleasant and the difficult.
Breathe into both with gentleness.

Expand your awareness now to hold both
your difficulty and your gratitude,
so wide you have space for both,
without pushing away one
or clinging to the other.
Even wider,
take in the unpleasant, the pleasant,
and all your body sensations.
Wider still to the room,
your surroundings.
Open to include the building or natural setting,
your neighborhood,
your town, your region.
The difficulty may not have changed,
but now it is part of something bigger.
If possible, let your gaze
encompass the wider world,
noticing that others are feeling
the same kind of pain.

You are not alone.
See the whole earth,
seamless, whole, precious.
Stay here for as long as you need.

When you are ready
—and you know this best—
slowly return to your part of this same world,
to your body,
to your sensation of what is
right here, right now.
Rest deeply in your body and breathe.
Allow your discomfort
to be soothed by this breath.
When you come to the end and prepare to rise,
see if you can carry a fresh sense
of this curiosity and kindness
to all you encounter.

This ends the Difficulties Meditation.

Lake Meditation

Lay down.
Pour the weight of your body
onto a surface you trust.
Sense comfort in being received—
head, shoulders, elbows,
the back of your upturned hands,
buttocks, calves, heels.
If you can, let go further,
the puddle of your tension
easing outward at the edges.
Drop deeper into quiet,
sink below the surface of things,
down, down,
past the layers of clarity,
into cooler, darker waters,
down, down,
until at last you come to rest
on the same basin of the earth
that holds openly and patiently
the wholeness of this mystery.
These waters teem with life
unseen by those above.
They undulate with freedom, calm,
and confidence,
knowing they are gently
yet firmly contained.
Steady enough to mirror sky and shore,
or to accept wind-swept,
turbulent, frozen,
the lake embodies noble ways
of being true waters,
adapting to surface things
and remaining as they are
deep, deep below.

This ends the Lake Meditation.

V
CONTRADICTIONS
explorations of the wholistic interplay between opposites
—joy and sorrow, clarity and confusion

Jury Duty

Formation begins
when a summons lands
amid bills and coupons.

You have no choice but to
frump at inconvenience
or muse on civic duty.

You do as you're told,
clearing your calendar
and weighing options for parking.

You expend false certainty
by telling yourself and friends
you'll never be called.

You show up on time,
believing their warning
that the deputy will find you.

You recall bits from
that class in government
as the jury officers starts training.

You picture free time
reading and working
while lawyers settle things out.

But you are called for the first case,
questioned with the first batch,
and seated on the jury by noon.

You heed the judge's insistence—
a presumption of innocence so strong
that the defense need not even speak.

You note the interplay
between systems and humanness
when jurors soon after talk lunch options.

Any citizen-become-juror,
confronted with meth-rotted lives
and a fully-emptied clip,

must lean on every step
from summons to verdict
as formation for deliberation—

Truth or something murkier?
Self-defense or murder?
All rise.

Brighter Day

Jim Croce sings with costly hope,
"Tomorrow's gonna be a brighter day."
Sure, we might look toward the next sunrise,

But what if it's 8:00 AM?
Can we surrender a whole day of moments,
rushing them past, wagering on tomorrow?
What might yet change this day?

Sleep for one. Maybe rest will restore
the body that carries us.
Beauty, too. Or being awakened
by the unexpected.

On the darkest days, though,
we cannot consciously direct our gaze.
Those are times we can't mumble,
let alone sing.

In those moments, any real hope
lies in memory of hard days endured,
of darkness loosed in hindsight.

Points of fact:

1. Jim Croce released the song "Tomorrow's Gonna Be a Brighter Day"
    in 1972 and died in a plane crash on Sept. 20, 1973.

2. Upon completing the first draft of this poem, I spilled my
    half-full coffee cup into my computer bag.

River Ways

What is it about the river
that makes me point the bow upstream
and paddle entirely
against nature's flow?

I kneel into the belly,
leaning deep into each pull,
feeling my back's power
—for the first little while.

Then comes deep fatigue,
and I pull against fears of letting up,
pulling more and harder,
afraid to lose all momentum.

Without force of my will
I will be pressed sideways,
wind and water moving my craft
like a sail on the river's whim.

Sometimes, I wonder about letting go
to sink a light stroke here and there,
to become content enough
with pointing my keel downstream.

Still Framed Wood

The windowed canvas of leafless woods
appears finished—until my eyes rest.

Scattered scurries of squirrels and birds
stir the branches to life.

Settle with any or stay with the whole—
but darting eyes makes me dizzy.

Like softer eyes see stars flicker,
a gentle gaze better perceives.

Acceptance
for Fr. Michael

Between stories of falling
near the bridge or at the altar,
followed by test after test,
came hints of hope and gratitude.

Diminishment compounds
when clippers slip weakened hands,
the choired voice trembles,
and once strong knees wobble.

Still, he speaks to 100 people
of awe at the human body
and appreciation for curious
and talkative physicians.

What gives him hope?
"I would find life itself
intolerable without faith and love
—regardless of my ALS."

What gives him strength?
"The is no cure for this disease,
so I pray for the grace to accept
what I have to accept."

Worn by the world's noise,
we listen enchanted
by strong vulnerability,
hungry to share such courage
with death before our eyes.

Steady One
for Beth

Quiet and steady she
rests only in the between—
patients and families,
family and aging,
siblings and questions,
kids and dreams,
critters and feed.

Rare is the stillness
to notice and feel
the heart's weight.
Moving from losses to needs
asks so much so often
it's hard to find her want.

So she evening walks
and tub soaks her way
through the middles,
quiet spaces
just for a breath,
just for herself.

Trust the Sun

for Will

"let us lay aside every weight . . . and run with perseverance . . ."
(Hebrews 12:1)

Some days the heart turns
partly cloudy with
a fair chance for drizzle.
Be unafraid,
for even the Master wept.
We live a hope
wide enough to
hold every experience.

However you feel, know this—
the Lord accompanies you
with all that you need—
healing, strength, belonging
beyond what you
even know to desire.
Trust the sun always
steady behind the clouds.

More Than Confidence

for Dei

"I can do all things through Christ who strengthens me."
(Philippians 4:13)

Confidence sounds
too thin a word
to claim what swells
within a heart
strengthened by God.
Your becoming began
before you knew
and will live on after
your every success
has wafted away.
So when you wonder
if . . . or but . . .
let those doubts blow
like leaves across the grass.
Hold firm to this—
God's strength,
planted in you
with cosmic love,
dwells so deeply in you
that you cannot resist
branching to the skies.

A Face Alive
for Michael

Some faces pass a day
with eyebrows knit
and teeth clenched,
plowing past joy
toward tomorrow.

Little has the power
to change them except
a chance encounter
with a face
alive

One that has learned
to follow love,
to cherish oneness,
to carry a sparkle
in the eyes.

Then, if scrunched faces
relax enough to smile
in return
they, too, can practice
awakening

To sun on the cheek,
to birdsong and persons,
to contentment
with today's life
really lived.

I Know

for Dawn
"surely I know the plans I have for you . . ."
(Jeremiah 29:11)

I know
I know
what you cannot see,
the things that can
and will be
on the other side
of your fears,
your doubts,
your questions.
I know
I know
who you are
and just how
I want to bless you
and help you grow.
I know
I know
that your hope,
your future,
are with me.
I will let you
find me so
you know
you know.

VI
LABORS
reminders of the dignity of human work
and the formation that accompanies it

Level-ish

Level-ish proves
a contradiction
just as plumb and square
can't mean "close enough."
Level is the only
sure foundation
for any stone or brick.
From pyramids to condos,
level holds the reference
for any at the craft.
So, in the moment when
the bubble is "just a tich off,"
what imbalance
leads me to shrug and press on?
What makes me concede
to this imperfection
and the next?
Whether hurry, clumsy,
or want of mindfulness,
every future cut will bear witness
to this moment's choice.
The line is not
a suggestion.

Lessons in Tiling

I once remodeled a bathroom so cute your knees hit the tub when seated. Having chipped off three decades of pink plastic tile and busted out the plaster beneath, I found "paper roll" in cursive, penciled onto a stud by some framer from 1939. Out with corroded steel pipe and in with new, up with patched walls, and then snapping a single level line around every wall, a line that will hold the weight of every first impression. I started in the corner behind the door, wanting to relearn how to tile somewhat out of view. For example, one must work to remember that all rows should be pinned to an edge or a baseboard while the glue sets. I realized this lesson in the morning when I found more than a few tiles drooping and dried below the level line. I could have paused or replaced them, but I told myself I'd just cover the margin with grout and then plowed through two more mornings of drooping tile on other walls. I even tried to act surprised. These days the sagging lines behind the door still testify to my first mistake. Those above the sink and covering the framer's careful script, on the other hand, will remain signs of my impatience for the next generation.

Chicken Coop Saga

Six years into the project, I have given over more weekends, blisters, timbers, and screws to an old bent coop than I can measure. The previous owner had said, "I put this up in a weekend," but I didn't hear that well enough to translate: "Burn it down now." Instead, one cumbersome cut at a time, I've added studs, rafters, and beams to brace a 3-D trapezoid. When it came to fixing the flooring boards that cracked further with every step, all I had on hand was milled red oak. So, I laid quartersawn under chicken shit. That's about right. No wall is square, daylight still shows through, and I've found karma in my complaint. When I extended the chicken run in a weekend, I set one post fully six inches off the mark. That beauty now serves as a constant reminder—I'm just the next previous owner.

Rule of Thirds

Some folks swing a magnet
over inches of bench debris,
in search of an unstripped screw.
Their chisels are dulled,
their rulers and pencils lost,
boxes of band-aids stacked nearby.

Better carpenters work in equal thirds—
first preparing a workspace,
then attending to the project itself,
finally clearing and resetting the shop.
There is sacrament and safety in this,
with far less angst and repair.

Novices protest the extra time
the Rule of Thirds requires,
gambling they'll avoid mistakes.
Wiser ones have learned
ease within these rhythms
and the secret to not starting over.

Milling a Timber

A sharp blade, well-aligned,
whispers through a log
until tree becomes board.

A dull blade, only slightly off,
drags, wanders, and waves,
pressing harder for far less true.

Other things go amiss, too,
like tiny set screws lost in the dirt,
or too little fluid in this or that.

In a moment glitches can compound,
sawdusting heartwood
seventy-five springs old.

What makes a sawyer, then,
is not speed or brawn
but well-earned humility.

Loyal to level and to legacy,
a good sawyer practices
making only one mistake at a time.

Natural Agency

a found poem from a
woodland stewardship magazine

Giving up to seek approval?
That under-stewards
our natural agency.
Watch and listen
when love and thrill are home.
Know the woods
need caretaking.
See eye to eye.
Do common ground.
Pour over and walk
every inch.
Decide on a plan.
Find help
and grow vital
trees standing 30, 40 feet tall.
Look to others
who seek, who love,
who anticipate.
Love a place
into perpetuity.

Eyes on the One

for David

"let us run with perseverance the race that is set before us . . ."
(Hebrews 12:1-2)

There is a moment in the blocks
when you can't see past the waiting,
eyes pressed down alongside
your fingers on the line.
Speed coiled in each sinew.
Ears and lungs wide open.
This moment is every bit
as much race as the run,
stretching your senses and focus
before you can see the destination.
This too is endurance,
persevering in patience,
in hope, in confidence.
Hold still, channel
your training, your thrill.
When the pistol cracks,
you must run, run,
fixing your eyes on the One.

Inestimably Many Dreams
for Dei

Imagine the tragedy
if each person had
only one shot, one race,
one song, one canvas,
one single attempt
among all their days
to achieve their thing.
Before the thing,
nothing but pressure.
After the thing, emptiness.

Better you and your
fascination with dreams
that animate your days
with curiosity, whimsy,
comingling passions.
Each a new challenge,
drawing out from you
something else
unexpected.

Your dreams breathe
in unfolding conversation
with who you are,
testing the facets
of your becoming.
To befriend the mysteries
of your being and to hone
even better gifts for the world,
live yes to each dream
that cascades into the next.

VII
LONGINGS
stirring desires for purpose, connection,
and mutual understanding all too often unspoken

Closer Still

Brow to earlobe,
shoulder to elbow,
hip to knee,
toe to knee—
Lovers stretching
the bounds of time,
each touch
an eternal choice
between close
and closer still.

Together and Apart
for Thomas and Ken

For those practicing love
there is a togetherness
so obvious
it contains being apart.

A cloud of birds rises,
paired wings take flight.
An ovation of trees stands
from single seeds and fifty springs.

Sand grains to beaches,
droplets to oceans,
pixels to rainbows,
snowflakes to white mornings.

So one beautiful love
unites two singular people
beyond any quaint notion
of proximity.

Togetherness glows
as one sun among galaxies,
at once near and far,
seen and unseen, always, always.

Remember

These words caress you
when I cannot,
simple as fingertips
drawn down your neck,
tender as kisses
between your breasts,
fierce as a sunrise gaze.
These words lead your hair
behind your ear,
peel off your woolen socks,
savor your every
delicate curve,
embrace you chest to chest.
These words will always
come home to your lips.
As nearness becomes
desire fulfilled,
these words breathe
warmly upon your skin,
again and again,
helping you remember.

Red Root 1

Touch a tree
and draw energy
from a wise keeper
of Creation's story.

Sense balance
and belonging,
even absent natural
perfection.

Tap into rootedness
before dawn,
after the storm-crush,
beyond the human toll.

Sink into underground branches,
embrace soil and loam.
Reach high and wide
toward a dignity not borrowed.

Be rooted and free.
Belong.
Be abundant.

Red Root 2

We are rooted in the earth.
We are grounded and free.
We stand supported and strong.
We are open, calm, worthy.
We weather fierce storms.
We are night's sentries.
We are not alone.
We are moved by birdsong.
We trust hints of dawn.
We are alive, flexible, loving, conscious.
We see truth.
We accept the unknown.
We welcome organic change.
We are abundant and free.
We are rooted in the One.

Still Point

for Jayce
"This is the way; walk in it . . ."
(Isaiah 30:21)

Behind every face
you wear for the world,
beneath every complex
motivation,
there is a still point.
A still point.

This inner place
is grounded, secure,
trustworthy.
It waits for the word
and listens for the Spirit.

Sometimes, duty and
busy-busy
make the still point
hard to find.
Wait for it.
Wait for it.

Your ears will hear
a holy nudge
through song, story,
conversation;
through woods, fields,
waters; through beautiful things
and beautiful people.

When you feel the still point
deep, deep within,
listen.
Listen to this way.
Run toward it.
Walk in it.

Taproot

after "Sink into the Taproot of Your Heart"
in *Turning Toward the Mystics* with James Finley

The tyranny of fear lives not
in the ordinary and necessary
instinct for survival,
but in its reverberations.
Trust the first fear,
the one shocked
by collective trauma
and uncertainty.
Beware the fears that follow,
those compounding
and clouding the first,
for overwhelmed hearts
can lose their source of courage,
become scattered,
diminished.
When that center fails
and the only choice seems
to withdraw, enflame,
or get swept away,
we must seek a deeper,
more durable
centering point.
Let us sink our taproots
into deathless beauty,
find ground near endless,
abiding love.
There, befriending the healing
forces of intimacy,
we will be ready to enter
the real fear as we are—
at once vulnerable and safe.

Watch Wood
for Russ and Dori

Too long has life pulled me away
from the sacred place I built—
a simple chair surrounded
by oak, walnut, ash, and pine.

Give me a moment to watch wood,
to trace again the grain with my eyes,
where sugars pulsed up and down
and cambium marked a season done.

Let me follow the wall's familiar paths
and winsome detours
where branch-knots carve shadows
into tall runs of heartwood.

Like these boards shaped into
something enduring,
show me again how to
slow down and come home.

Bring me back to the days
of sun-washed canopy,
hard-breathing up the bluffs
to taste fresh air, sweat, and dust.

Help me remember
the ache of sacred work—
bringing in timbers, opening joints,
lifting beams into a quiet crypt

That I may heed the call
to natural kinship,
a cleansing invitation to pause
and begin noticing again.

VIII
WONDERS
encounters with awe and reverence
that leave us humbled and free

Whisper
for Dawn

From beneath the busyness
comes a whispered call to adventure.
You may choose not to speak it
for Mom's sake or Dad's,
or to avoid making friends
and siblings feel left out.
Still the whisper persists,
calling you toward a journey
only you can make.
These are the natural
and necessary
rhythms of adulting.
Some days the warmth
of celebration
will mingle with coolness
at the changing of things.
That's what the whisper is for,
a holy reminder that the
winds of unconditional love
are filling your sails.

Snowed Forest

Fresh heavy snows
reveal woodland mysteries
naturally hidden.
White-dustings
and sagging branches
now draw the eye.
A cedar top
bent over itself,
snapped at the middle.
Red oaks and osier dogwoods
stand out like flames.
Unseen but for a blanket of hints,
black chickadee caps bobbing,
footpaths crossed earlier
by a slow old buck,
ancient hollows in still older walnuts,
all eagerly whisper
to a world quiet at last.

Questions Tumble

after "Grief is a Question"
by Kiely Todd Roska

Sometimes questions
tumble, tumble
through her everything,
soul wrestling
unwanted truth.
Not to seek quick answers
or short-lived relief,
but to exercise ocean waves
of love-soaked grief.
Why, why, WHY?
meets a grandchild's,
"Can you love after you die?"
while she still wonders
whether to serve
the carrots and horseradish
only her mother loved.
Somehow,
this act of questioning
becomes itself
raft and beacon,
means of life on immense,
unending waters.

Joy Complete

for Dad

"make my joy complete: be of the same mind, having the same love . . ."
(Philippians 2:1-2)

Some are born
convinced
that more joy
lies ahead.
Waking, sleeping,
they dream.
With every
What if . . .
they take God's hand
and lean toward
the horizon.
What if . . .
love and
tenderness
were to unite us?
What if . . .
we followed
the way of most
compassion?
What if . . .
God was born
with a mind like this,
and dreaming itself
means complete
and holy joy?

To Be Open

with thanks to Maria Tattu Bowen

Too many stories are rolling in
like thunderstorms,
beginning on ominous horizons
and reaching an eerie quiet
when the critters first hide.
Winds press in, skies dim,
and drops of words
growing heavier
eventually soak us to the bone.
It's hard to keep listening
to this season of humanity
without any clear sign
we can simply wait it out.
To remain open—
to shelter enough
that we navigate storms,
rather than chasing or fleeing them—
look through the clouds,
practice joy for the sorrow,
breath for the exhaustion,
kinship for the loneliness,
accord for the division,
and creation for the breakdowns.
The eye of every storm,
and that which will turn this season,
can and must be rituals of life
that refuse to shutter the last window.

She Holds Mystery

The Black Madonna of St. Paul's Monastery

The Black Madonna
keeps a liturgy of all hours
in these monastic halls.
Proud, patient, whole
she stands,
waiting for all who come.
Pass her by,
brisk or burdened,
and you will miss her
steadfast witness.
"Listen . . ."
Mary seems to whisper,
leaning toward
the Cosmic Mystery
she cradles in her arms.

Spacious

after *Our Unforming* by Cindy Lee

To allow a question
to remain unanswered
and to dwell there
until freedom comes,
cultivate spaciousness
like mystics.
Expect no straight lines.
Listen for wisdom
beyond the mind.
Distrust any solitude
that discounts its essential
bond to all living things.
With contemplative hearts
and hope for congruence,
let us accompany
one another in joy,
sorrow, and uncertainty,
practicing our way
toward a posture of
simultaneous,
collective healing.

ABOUT THE AUTHORS

S amuel Rahberg is a spiritual director, CliftonStrengths coach, and retreat facilitator who has been engaging with the themes of this collection personally and as a companion for decades. He is a spouse and father of two adult children. His titles include *Ice Break: Poems about Change* (Aetos Publications, 2019), *Enduring Ministry: Toward a Lifetime of Christian Leadership* (Liturgical Press, 2017), and several volumes on the Gospels in poems and image, which were created in collaboration with Natalie Adebiyi. For the joy of encountering God in nature, his family stewards a woodland retreat in Southeast Minnesota. Samuel also serves as Director of the Certificate in Spiritual Direction at Saint John's School of Theology (Collegeville, MN), where he earned an M.A. in Theology.

www.samuelrahberg.com

N atalie Adebiyi collaborates with commercial and residential patrons and designers to create unique artwork, transform spaces, and market to customers. She studied in Italy as a member of the National Society of Collegiate Scholars. Her work has been exhibited at the Dallas Museum of Art and in numerous juried shows. When not collaborating with others, she spends time with her family, gardens, volunteers, and paints.

www.paintingsandmurals.com

www.ingramcontent.com/pod-product-compliance
Lightning Source LLC
Chambersburg PA
CBHW071133090426
42736CB00012B/2108